50 QUESTIONS TO ASK

Before & After You Say

"I Do"

Make your Heaven on earth with the Love of your life building an unshakable companionship on the solid foundation of Love & Wisdom.

- *Uché Kay-Giourtzis*

50+ Questions to Ask before and after you say "I Do"

For permission requests, e-mail coach@uchekay.com with the subject matter 'Attention - Permissions Request'

Ordering information:

www.uchekay.com

Cover designed by: Izabela Designs

Illustrations by Muhammad Asad Ullah

Edited by Udoka Ohuonu, Lynne Mcfarlane

TLC Publishing

ISBN: 9798454514426

Formatted by: Alo-Timeys

Visit our website at www.uchekay.com

CONTENTS

DEDICATION

Dedicated to my first husband, J.C., who loved me with a Selfless love.

And even gave up His life for mine all in a bid to Keep me alive!

Thank you,

I am still living, Because of YOU!!!

I owe it to you to live my best life ever, thank you for a Second chance at living life to the full.

Every day is an opportunity to live

Better than the day before, always being and doing the best I can!

FOREWORD

In a time where culture norms about marriage are constantly shifting, Uché Kay brings us a light-hearted, yet much needed resource, on preparing to stay grounded as you embark on one of the most important decisions of your life.

In 50+ Questions, Uché encourages couples to engage in reflection, dialogue, and action, in order to address crucial issues that can often be overlooked when entering into marriage.

Applying a fun, yet sober approach, Uché tackles a wide range of topics to help couples build a solid foundation on which to begin and sustain their marriage. It's a resource that doesn't take long to read, but if this book is used in the way that it has been intended, then the long-term impact of it and the fruit produced, has the potential to be a great blessing to your marital adventure.

Bobbi Kumari
Author of Sacred Sexuality – Rewire Your Desire
Towards True Intimacy
www.livinginlight.co.uk/sacred-sexuality

ACKNOWLEDGMENT

Ioannis Giourtzis my Love, treasured and cherished Husband, number one fan and prime-mover, because of you I have healed in so many ways and still continue to build my wholesomeness; together you whole plus me whole we make a super-dynamic Power-House!

My Mothers Anne Omorogbe and Paraskevi Giourtzi. My blood Rosabella Efe (representing) and Okeremute Ijoma. Pastors Fred and Kanmi Igho, Samson and Ope Jedafe and Rod and Julie Anderson. Abiola Dikko, Bobbi Kumari, Ralph Watson, Robert Robert, Margaret Kasim, Bola Fadahunsi, Lynne Mcfarlane, Selina Bishop-Gooding, Udoka Ohuonu, Emma Emmanuel, Kristina Ukhuegbe,

Belle Scott, Christina Roberts, Cristiane DeSousa.

Thanking you all so very much from the depths of my heart.

It is impossible to thank everyone who has helped me share my message and I therefore apologise to all my fans, supporters, affiliates, friends, and relatives who are not listed here. I would like you to know however, that I emphatically thank you for your graciousness and for all the ways you have been there for me, I appreciate you.

REVIEWS

"It's a very good and quick read; the direct list of questions is also very good and deeply thought provoking."

- Julie Anderson, Senior Leader: Commonwealth Christian Fellowship CCF

"An informative compilation, with practical questions that set the foundation of relationship you intend to be in for the long haul. A good work-type-book. I would recommend this easy read to any contemplating marriage or a long-term relationship as well as singles who plan to one day spend the rest of their lives with someone special"

*-Bobbi Kumar,
CEO Living in Light and Author of Sacred Sexuality*

"A highly informative and useful read; I would recommend to anyone either considering or about to enter into the lasting commitment of marriage – or any form of a long-term relationship. Uché lays it all out in simple terms and plain language that I'm sure the reader will appreciate."

-Ralph Watson,
Coach, Personal Development Specialist and Author.

"This short book is an essential read before you commit to a long-term relationship. It will open your eyes to enable you to get that wonderful love for life that you deserve."

–Bob Roberts,
MBE, Master Coach Master NLP Trainer, Therapist,
and International Management Consultant

"Uché, this is a truly amazing book

and certainly a must read for every couple before they tie the knot!

It's a 'necessity' not a 'want'! Well done!

Your obedience to this call will prevent anyone reading this book from going into marriage unprepared. That's how seriously we should take our calling. Someone's life could depend on it...

God bless and reward your obedience!"

–*Emma M Emmanuel LLM*
Human Rights Lawyer, Author

Having been married for over 21 years and active in the marriage counselling ministry for over 16 years, we find this well researched and a hundred percent practical book, "50 Questions to Ask before and after you say "I do" by Uché Kay-G. is a great manual for life. Uché has put in so much experience in this project to help any reader from repeating the mistakes of failed marriages. So, it's a book to carry with you and not to stow away on the shelf.

–*Fred and Kanmi IGHO*
Overseer of KLM, Founder of the School of Ministry

INTRODUCTION

With the high rate of divorce in our society, this book aims at encouraging couples to enter Holy Matrimony with a lot more intention and respect.

It covers many areas, including Sex and Money, which are reported to be among the top ten most common causes and reasons for divorce.

"I have had enough, I want a divorce," shouted Harry!

Carrie cried as her heart sank; her knees buckled beneath her, and she slumped to the floor, barely allowing her a graceful fall. She knew Harry really meant it this time. Before marriage Carrie was extremely excited for them to be wedded. They had been arguing on and off for about two years into the marriage without genuinely getting to the bottom of their misunderstandings. Harry's financial status now less buoyant than in times past had gradually left him sensitive, insecure, and less tolerant. His conversations with Carrie if any had become short, abrupt, and spiteful. All she could muster to say was, "I wish we got to know each other better before we started having sex".

The above scenario is the experience for some couples. At first, they are head over heels "in love" with each other, and only see the cracks in the relationship after it is far too late to save it.

Before you choose a job, a course in university, or buy a house, typically, some sort of research and effort needs to go into getting a favourable end result.

It is no different from having a lasting marriage. I believe it is possible to be happy with the same spouse until death do you both part. You can even be more in love in your old age than when you first met, and the relationship was still new and exciting.

I lay no claim to being the final authority on marriage, but from experience, years of research and insights, I have compiled in this booklet more than 50 hard-core, life-changing, and transformative questions you should ask before you tie the knot!

The list can serve and save any partnership if the couple are open and willing to give the questions true, sincere, and heartfelt answers. This list is by no means exhaustive, but the questions endeavour to uncover any potential "red flags" and issues that can make or break any union, both before and after marriage.

Even if you are already married these questions can be used to review your current state as a couple. When areas that require adjustments are replaced with deliberate steps and progressive actions to improve them, the results will certainly favour the health of your relationship. It is like an annual car service. The checks highlight any problems to be addressed which, once corrected, the performance of your vehicle will be enhanced. The moment a car leaves the showroom its value depreciates, and it is no longer "brand new". Similarly, beyond

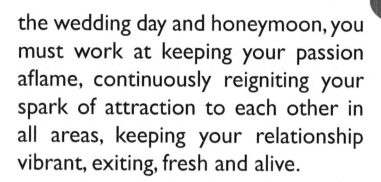

the wedding day and honeymoon, you must work at keeping your passion aflame, continuously reigniting your spark of attraction to each other in all areas, keeping your relationship vibrant, exiting, fresh and alive.

Marriage courses are a great help in preparing couples for their life together. One that comes highly recommended by marriage officiants, including Rod Anderson–co-founder of Prayer for the Nations and CCF – Commonwealth Christian Fellowship - Senior Pastor, (he joined my husband and I in Holy matrimony) is "The Marriage Preparation Course" [1].

The course was founded and is conducted by none other than Nicky and Sila Lee of Holy Trinity Brompton. Together they created and deliver this profoundly comprehensive course. They also created The Marriage Course for married couples. Both courses can be enrolled in by couples of any background, faith, or race in the UK and internationally.

My Husband and I had the privilege of enrolling for the course and completing it. It helped us to bond more and develop a deeper understanding of each other on several levels.

It is my utmost desire that you and your partner connect and truly become as one flesh.

As important as marriage is, very few couples purposefully plan towards having and enjoying an ongoing, exceedingly successful union. Consciously searching out relevant wisdom will make your relationship flourish, grow continuously, and remain permanent.

It is one of life's greatest gifts to share your life with another and genuinely experience companionship, joy, and love on a deep, high, and intimate level.

So, enjoy the questions in this book! Use them as a guide to explore and build on your existing relationship. If you are already married, reword the questions accordingly to suit you, and review them periodically.

Happy co-mingling!!!

- Uché Kay-Giourtzis

LOVE

1.   What is your definition of love?

2.   With love as the dictating factor, is there anything you cannot forgive in our union?

According to Gary Chapman[2], The

Five Love Languages are receiving gifts, quality time, words of affirmation, acts of service and physical touch. With five as the highest and one the least, in what order would you list these five languages for yourself?

3. Explain what love is to you! After, I will tell you what love means to me; What adjustments do you feel are required of us to remain in love with each other until our final days on earth?

4. How can we keep our love fresh, new, and exciting even after being together for many years?

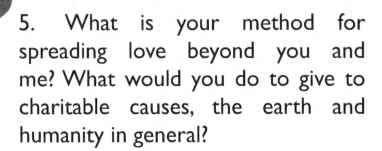

5. What is your method for spreading love beyond you and me? What would you do to give to charitable causes, the earth and humanity in general?

The Ancient Greek Philosophy expands the one word "LOVE", breaking it into what you could describe as branches, and stretches its explanation more broadly to include the following concepts: *Agápe*[3] – unconditional love, *Éros*[4] – romantic/ erotic love, *Philia*[5] – friendship, *Storge*[6] – parental love, *Philautia*[7] – self-compassion and *Xenia*[8] - hospitality. Love encompasses all these as essential ingredients where without them it is like an unbalanced scale, or a wholesome homemade meal but

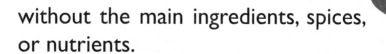

without the main ingredients, spices, or nutrients.

My conclusion, we Humans are Spirits with a soul, living in a body, and to be healthy, whole, and complete we must nurture and nourish ALL three – Spirit, Soul and Body. Likewise, the above named and all branches of love are necessary for living Life generally and especially as couples, or individuals in a relationship.

HEALTH

"Cleanliness is next to godliness" and "Health is Wealth"!

6.   What standards in relation to our health, hygiene, general welfare and cleanliness are of utmost or no

importance to you?

7.　The general marital vows include "in sickness and in health". The ideal things to do are exercising to maintain fitness, eating right, and having faith to live in good health. If there were severe health issues, what would you do to show your commitment and dedication to our union and me?

8.　How vital are exercise and diet to you? How often do you exercise and what does your diet consist of?

9.　What health matters in your family should I be made aware of?

10. In some cultures, and religions, blood transfusion is a complete "no, no"! What are your views on giving and receiving blood, and how would this or affect us?

11. In the 2020, the face of the Earth was shockingly swept over with covid19; many have received vaccines some have not, what difference (if any) would it make between us? What is the ultimate resolution for us as a couple be it this pandemic's jab, such like or any other future vaccines?

FINANCES

12. How much money do you earn?

13. What are the benefits of a having a joint account or an Accountant and

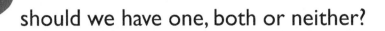

should we have one, both or neither?

14.   What account(s) can we agree on to best address the overall budgeting of our home, a joint account, separate personal accounts, or both? How often should we review our finances?

15.   What percentage of your income will you contribute to the upkeep of the home and what percentage will you keep for yourself?

16. How best can we unite our finances to agree on the best distribution of our resources as a family unit?

LIFESTYLE

17. Where would you like to live, and what are the must-haves for the family home?

18. What do you do in your leisure time? Some consider smoking, alcohol, and recreational drugs as agents of relaxation. How do you see these and how important are they to you to have or not to have?

19. What precisely do you consider to be leisure and pleasure and how much importance are these to you?

20. How much time would you give to leisure? How much time for relaxation pleasure must you have

21. Can you drive - What is your preparedness for ANY situation requiring urgent attention/

emergencies? (Be creative and think of any realistic emergency to demonstrate your answer).

22. Do you swear and use foul language, would you like to stop?

If yes, in times of frustration or anger have you considered if you used the actual words such as 'sex' opposed to the 'f' word for example, and real names of the human genitalia, that that would help keep you light-hearted?

This suggestion is posed to help balance your emotions. Simply thinking about using the word 'sex' and reproductive organs to replace swear words should present some humour opposed to vexation, prevent high blood pressure, and preserve your state of tranquillity and peace.

CHILDREN AND OTHER FAMILY MEMBERS

23. Do you want children, if "yes" how many if "no" why? (If no, skip to question 31, and if 31 is not applicable skip to 32).

24. We all pray for healthy children. Today's technology is so advanced; we can see how healthy an unborn child is. If the Doctor detects a condition that will affect the child for life, what would your reaction be? What is your stance on abortion, would you commit to care for the baby providing the best quality of life possible no matter the difficulties?

25. What type of schools will our children attend? Would you consider homeschooling?

26. Will we have our children vaccinated?

27. Should we both want children but find this a challenge, would you consider IVF treatment – (in vitro fertilisation), adopt, or do all it takes or be happy and grow old without any offspring?

28. The loss of a child – miscarriage, as an infant, child, teen or adult is inexplicable,after such a life experience how would you work to help us heal as individuals and encourage the deepening of our relationship as a couple?

What would your reaction be to a pregnancy that we had no plans for, and will drastically change the status quo for life both short term and long term?

29. Some people believe in smacking children, even under the age of 18 months. Some people believe in allowing a baby who does not sleep easily to be left to cry under the "cry it out" method, while you time how long the child is left to cry! There are also other forms of discipline; What disciplinary practices were you brought up with and how would you like us to discipline our children and incorporate best behaviour in them? Do you believe in smacking and from what age?

30. How would you address the issue of sexuality or the sexual orientation of our child(ren) especially if it turns out different from what we expect or have trained them up to be?

31. Where children already exist from previous relationships, how would you adjust and step into being a parental figure for them, especially during the 'terrible twos' and the 'trying teenagers' years?

32. How much of our immediate, external family members or our in-laws may be a part of our home? What are acceptable boundaries? Would you like to have a pet?

SEX

For some reason sex is a topic that a lot of people feel most uncomfortable

talking about, yet nearly all people engage in sex. Some people use swear words (e.g., f****, or d***, c***, w***** and p****) that are related to sexual intercourse and to male and female private parts. It is interesting how such words are used in public with much vulgarity, insensitively, distastefully and without respect. All around the world it can be found that similar taboo or crass words are related to intercourse, male, and female genitalia but with a derogatory connotation, yet the sacredness of sex is hardly ever talked about.

A lot of people shy away from talking about it but easily indulge in the act of doing it. Sex is phenomenally powerful! Beyond the bodily effects, the spirit and soul of those involved are altered. It can harm and it can heal.

33. Do you like sex and how much of it would you genuinely be happy to partake in weekly or even daily? Do you have sexual fantasies? What

are the detrimental or edifying effects they can have on us? What happens if our interest in sex is disproportionate and one of us has more interest in sex than the other?.

34. Marriage is honourable, and the marital bed is to be undefiled by sex before marriage and any form of perverseness. What are your honest thoughts on fornication, adultery or threesomes and swinging?

35. What is your viewpoint on oral sex – 69, fellatio and cunnilingus? Would you give, receive or both? Why?

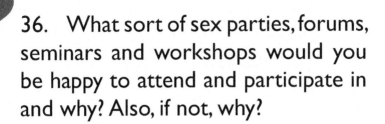

36. What sort of sex parties, forums, seminars and workshops would you be happy to attend and participate in and why? Also, if not, why?

Faith isn't just a notion that some people hold onto in tough times; faith is an important element to all human life on earth. Life is precious, but it can also be remarkably difficult at times. Faith is what helps to get us through, illuminating the pathway in times of darkness, helping to give us strength in times of weakness. Without faith, we are nothing.

FAITH

37. Please explain what having 'a faith' means to you. Do you believe in God a Divine Being or higher power or not?

38. How do you conquer life's challenges or triumph in opportunities

disguised as trouble? Are you a half full or half empty type person and why?

39.   Is God significant in all areas of your life and how much influence is God allowed in your life? If no, how do you maintain a spiritual balance?

40.   How many times a week would we attend the temple/ church/ synagogue/ mosque or whichever place of worship? Will we go as a couple/ as an entire family, or not at all? How important is this? Either way, consider the impact the effects could have on us, what could they be – to name a few, as many or all you can think of? If negative, how best can we address this?

41. What do you believe about the afterlife? Do you believe in the possibility of meeting after we transition from this sphere?

CAREER AND BUSINESS

42.   On what level of importance is career and business on in your life and how do you intend to balance them with our relationship?

43. How do you intend to keep both sides (career/business and us) 100% satisfied? Are there any things like bankruptcy, business, or personal debts that I need to be informed of? How best do we prevent any of such situations befalling us?

NATURE

44. What parts of creation do you enjoy, (e.g. sunset and or sunrise) if at all?

45 What is your version of tranquillity and how do you address stress, depression or low mood and anxiety?

46. Being close to nature can keep you centred, calm, rejuvenated and creative. What is your favourite aspect of nature? Is it something you would share with me, prefer to keep for yourself or depending on the time, both?

Where would you prefer to live in most days of your life?

HOLIDAYS

47. Where in the world are the places you would love to visit in your lifetime? The absolute must see(s)?!

48. What is your outlook on either of us traveling without each other, the children if we have any or traveling without each other but with other people e.g., friends, relatives, or work colleagues?

COMMUNICATION

The aim of this will be for us to skilfully develop our ability to effectively communicate with one another and ultimately converse opposed to argue.

Albert Mehrabian in his book - Silent Messages[9], details his findings on inconsistent messages of feelings and attitudes and the relative importance of words vs. nonverbal cues. The popular saying after all, is that:"actions speak louder than words". Mehrabian is the man renowned for the 7-38-55 formula; his research established situations where people's words did not match their facial expressions.

49. What would you consider to be your most effective mode of communication for us as a couple?

50. How best would you suggest after a heated argument that we iron out our differences in a RESPECTFUL

manner and to agree on the most suitable way to move forward together?

51. What times and places would you consider being the best to discuss matters that are extremely important to us?

52. Would you go to bed angry or upset with me? Do you allow unspoken issues to fester in malice, as opposed to discussing them openly? How would you describe yourself, like a stream or a violent tsunami?

53. Do you strike out at people, animals, or things – physically, verbally,

emotionally when you are highly frustrated? How could we best enhance self-control in ourselves or in each other?

DESTINY

Destiny[10] defined, is the force which some people believe controls the things that happen to you in life. Every life is connected to a purpose.

54. Do you know what you must 'by all means do' in your life and what strategies are in place to ensure that this happens in your lifetime?

THE WINTER YEARS OF LIFE

55. Planning to remain lovers, companions, and best friends to each other is the ideal aim. What can we do now to guarantee to the best of our abilities the highest likelihood of us

living well into our old age together?

56.   Some people enter into prenups, how best can we ensure that even with material things we will look out for each other's interests as we two become one?

57.   Some people look dimly on ageing, but it is certainly possible to view that stage of life as successful! What does successful ageing mean to you?

58.   Where would you wish to spend your winter years?

59.   Before some couples reach a

beautiful old age they write their will, relating this to our union, what do you consider would be the best idea for our relationship?

50+

Questions Asked

I expect that you are still passionately in love with each other. I suggest you write your answers down and review them ever so often.

CONGRATULATIONS!

REFERENCES

1. Lee, Nicky & Sila (2000). *The Marriage Preparation Course* – Alpha International HTB Brompton Road, London SW7 1JA. United Kingdom.

https://alpha.org.uk/the-marriage-courses

Tel: +44 (0)20 7052 0200

2. Chapman, G.D. (1992). *The 5 Love languages - How to Express Heartfelt Commitment to Your Mate.* Chicago: Northfield Pub., United States

3. Liddell, H.G.; Scott, R. (1994). *Agápē: An intermediate Greek-English Lexicon: Seventh Edition.* Oxford: Clarendon Press

4.   Soble, A. (1989). *Éros: Readings in the philosophy of Love. Sixth Edition.* New York, N.Y., Paragon House

5. Liddell, H.G.; Scott, R. (October 2010). *Philia - An intermediate Greek-English Lexicon: Founded upon the Seventh Edition of Liddell and Scott's Greek-English Lexicon.* Benediction Classics. P. 4 ISBN 978-1-84902-626-0

6. Liddell, H.G.; Scott, R. (1994). *Storge - An intermediate Greek-English Lexicon: Seventh Edition.* Oxford: Clarendon Press

7. Liddell, H.G.; Scott, R. (October

2010). *Philautia - An intermediate Greek-English Lexicon: Founded upon the Seventh Edition of Liddell and Scott's Greek-English Lexicon.* Benediction Classics. P. 4 ISBN 978-1-84902-626-0

8. Powell, A. (1995). *Xenia: The Greek World.* London, Routledge. ISBN 0-203-04216-6

9. Mehrabian, A. *(1971). Sixth Edition Silent Messages.* Belmont, California, Wadsworth Publishing Company

10. Harper Collins (1994). *Destiny*: Collins English Dictionary. Glasgow: Publishers.

DISCLAIMER

This compilation is gathered from interviews, years of experience, observations, and research made by me. I lay no claim to being the final authority in these matters. I assure that if the questions are answered with all honesty, they will 100% improve a once average relationship and bring it to an authentic fertile ground yielding productive results. Your union will blossom and induce a massive harvest for the both of you as individuals and for the relationship itself.

The choice to gain great results from these questions and how best to exercise them to your benefit is all yours, I trust you will use them well.

Uché Kay-Giourtzis can be contacted through the following platforms:

 https://uchekay.com/

 Email:coach@uchekay.com

 https://www.facebook.com/uchekay.life.relationship.coach/

 https://www.facebook.com/groups/751123845631728

 https://www.instagram.com/uchekay/

 https://www.youtube.com/channel/UCsREoVx3dpomxAatlqGpLmw/featured

NOTES

NOTES

NOTES

NOTES

NOTES

NOTES

NOTES

NOTES

NOTES

NOTES

NOTES

NOTES

NOTES

NOTES

NOTES

Printed in Great Britain
by Amazon